SCHOLASTIC'S A+ GUIDE TO RESEARCH and TERM PAPERS

LOUISE COLLIGAN

SCHOLASTIC INC.
New York Toronto London Auckland Sydney

Over a million junior high and high school students have used Scholastic's A + Guides to raise their grades, do better in every subject, and *enjoy* school more. Now you can, too!

SCHOLASTIC'S A +
GUIDE TO GOOD GRADES

SCHOLASTIC'S A +
GUIDE TO GOOD WRITING

SCHOLASTIC'S A +
GUIDE TO TAKING TESTS

SCHOLASTIC'S A +
GUIDE TO GRAMMAR

SCHOLASTIC'S A +
GUIDE TO RESEARCH AND TERM PAPERS

SCHOLASTIC'S A +
GUIDE TO BOOK REPORTS

ISBN 0-590-33317-8

12 11 10 9 8 7 6 5   7 8/8

To Doug and Deirdre

CONTENTS

Chapter 5. RESEARCH PAPER SURVIVAL KIT

Chapter 1

WHAT'S THE BIG IDEA: Finding a Topic and Getting Started

For generations, the announcement of a research or term paper has struck dread in the hearts of countless students. Most have a few vague notions about what a research paper is: it's long; it's probably boring; it involves trips to the library; and, thank goodness, it's not due for six weeks. But those six weeks (or four or eight, depending on your teacher's deadline) have a way of disappearing fast.

Research papers aren't assigned to make your life miserable or keep you up nights. Like the work you do on other school assignments, putting together a research paper helps you develop skills you'll be using in college or in a future job.

1

You gather information on a particular subject from several sources. You put the information together. And you write up your impressions of what all that information means. If you have ever written a business letter, book report, essay, lab report, or short social studies paper, then you've run through several of these steps already. In a research paper, however, you are expected to tackle a larger subject over a longer period of time than you've allotted for previous writing assignments.

To make your job easier, there's a standard form that researchers, teachers, and scholars have developed for the research paper. This book will show you how to plan, organize, and write one according to this established form. Included in each chapter are one or more "Trying It Out" boxes. These instructions will help you apply the skills mentioned in the chapter to your actual paper. There is also a "Progress Check" section at the end of each chapter to help you determine any problem areas or goals you need to work on at that point.

While this guidebook doesn't come with the guarantee of an A+, it will help you do the best possible job on your research project in the most efficient way.

GETTING THE ASSIGNMENT

Your countdown begins from the moment your teacher announces that a research paper is due on a certain date. This announcement will probably be greeted with a lot of nervous shuffling and sighs. Once you've regained your wits, make sure you get these basic questions answered before you leave class:

- When is the assignment due?
- What is the purpose of the assignment?
- Do I choose my own topic or is one assigned?
- What exactly am I supposed to do?
- How long should the paper be?
- How many sources will be required?
- Are footnotes and a bibliography required?
- Does the paper have to be typed?
- In addition to the completed paper, must I also submit my outline and note cards?
- Is there a penalty for a late paper?

Chances are your teacher will hand out a sheet with all the specifications. If not, make sure you have a clear idea of the assignment before you get started. You'll save yourself a lot of headaches later on if you know exactly what is expected right from the beginning.

EQUIPPING YOURSELF FOR THE JOB

You'll be living with your research project for several weeks, so it's a good idea to set up a base of operations from which you can work. Nothing is more frustrating than getting all set to write and discovering that your note cards and outline are nowhere to be found. Here are a few tips for keeping the different parts of your project under control:

- Get a tote bag, a knapsack, a shopping bag, or even a laundry basket to store all your research materials.

- In your storage space, keep a large supply of scrap paper, pens, pencils, small index cards, and a steno pad or yellow legal pad.

- Have a dictionary and thesaurus on hand. You'll need these practical references when you get to the actual writing of your paper.

- Stake out a quiet corner of your bedroom as a work area. Keep your bagful of supplies, books, and notes there.

- Apply for a library card if you don't already have one. While your school library is probably the most convenient place to research your project, you may find twenty-five classmates competing for the same books and references you want. A card to your local public library gives you access to a larger selection of materials. Moreover, there will be less demand for popular references like the encyclopedia and *The Readers' Guide to Periodical Literature*.

- It's worth your while to get acquainted with a librarian. Introduce yourself to her on your first visit. She'll know all the shortcuts for finding what you need. A helpful librarian will give you a short tour of the facilities and show you how to use things like the card catalog, periodicals, and audio-visual or microfilm machines. Make your library visit early in your project so that you can get acquainted with a staff member and the facilities when you're not under the pressure of a fast-approaching deadline.

THE 10 BASIC STEPS AND SCHEDULE

The prospect of a research paper often looms like a large dark cloud over the heads of many students. A project this size can be intimidating if you try to take in all the different parts at once. So don't. Save yourself a lot of anxiety by looking at your paper as a series of small assignments rather than as one huge project.

Inevitably, some people wind up cramming their reserch paper into two or three days of intensive non-stop work. It can be done, but usually with disastrous results. There's an easier way to do the job, and here are ten steps that will whittle down your project to a systematic and manageable series of tasks:

1. **Choose a general subject area that interests you.**

2. **Narrow down your subject area to a specific topic.** Look for smaller subtopics within the major subject.

3. **Write a thesis statement that sums up your plan and main ideas for your paper.**

4. **Gather information in the library.** Conduct any surveys or personal interviews if you plan to use them as part of your paper.

5. **Take notes on index cards.** Record your research sources on bibliography cards and factual information and quotations on note cards.

6. **Write up an outline from your note cards.** Arrange your cards in a logical order that supports your thesis statement. Then transfer main ideas and subtopics from your sequential note cards to an outline.

7. **Write the first draft of your paper.** Use your note cards and outline as the framework for your first draft.

8. **Proofread and revise your first draft.** Work on matters of style and organization when you revise your draft. Check for errors and see that all your quotations and factual information are accurate.

9. **Write your final draft.** Rewrite your paper from the corrected first draft. Add footnotes, a bibliography page, and a title page.

10. **Assemble and proofread the final draft.** Make sure there are no mechanical errors. See that the paper is neat and readable. Submit it on or before the due date.

There you have it—the ten basic steps to writing a research paper. Think of each step as a small, separate assignment. Don't give a thought to your outline until you're comfortable with your subject. Forget about footnotes until you have a rough draft. Until you get to the proofreading stage, don't get too bogged down in grammar, spelling, and punctuation. If you move through your project in gradual steps, you'll get through the entire paper before you realize it.

Trying It Out

The best way to ensure that you tackle your research paper systematically is to work out a schedule for the project early on. You may want to coordinate with your teacher the mini-deadlines for each step along the way, or you may simply want to keep the schedule for your private use.

Goal:

To organize your research paper one job at a time.

Procedure:

Write the due dates in the blanks provided and check off each task as you complete it. (You'll find an extra schedule on page 111.)

Research

Jobs to be done: Due Dates: Check-off:

1. Think of a general subject that interests you.   ____ ____

2. Narrow your general subject down to a specific subtopic.   ____ ____

3. Go to the library and see what information is available on your topic. Make a list of all usable research sources on bibliography cards.   ____ ____

4. Take notes on the materials you listed. Record your research on note cards.   ____ ____

5. Write a thesis statement that sums up the main point of your paper and the research you have uncovered so far.   ____ ____

Organizing Your Paper

6. Read over your note cards and decide what information you would like to include or omit. ____ ____

7. Arrange your note cards in logical order. ____ ____

8. Write an outline based on the arrangement of your note cards. ____ ____

Writing Your Paper

9. Write a rough draft of your paper, main point by main point, from your outline and note cards. Support each main idea with facts, examples, and subtopics from your note cards. ____ ____

10. Work on the introduction and conclusion of your paper. ____ ____

11. Go over your rough draft to see if all your ideas relate to one another and to

your thesis state-
ment. Check that
you've supported all
your main ideas with
researched facts and
examples. Polish the
style of your rough
draft.   ____   ____
12. Rewrite your
rough draft into a fi-
nal copy. Document
facts, quotations, and
passages with foot-
notes. Write up a bib-
liography sheet from
your bibliography
cards.   ____   ____
13 Proofread your fi-
nal draft for mechan-
ics and neatness.   ____   ____
14. Submit your pa-
per on the due date.   ____   ____

STEP 1: CHOOSE A GENERAL SUBJECT AREA THAT INTERESTS YOU

In planning a research paper, there's one step
you can't postpone—choosing your topic. Even
if you attempt to write your entire paper the day

before it's due, finding a workable topic takes some preliminary legwork.

What makes a subject worth writing about? Here are a few things to consider when you start looking around for the right topic:

• Find a subject you're familiar with. Are you an expert on television trivia? A baseball nut? A comic-book collector? A budding poet? A whiz in physics or biology? The easiest paper to write is one dealing with a subject about which you already know.

• Explore an area you would like to learn more about. Maybe you've always had a passing interest in the Wild West but never had time to read up on it. This may be a chance to turn your interest into a real investigation.

• Pay a short visit to the library to determine if there's enough suitable information there to make a particular topic worth exploring further. A well-researched paper needs at least five or six different sources. Can you locate at least a few books on the subject that interests you? Are there two or three magazine or newspaper articles about the topic? If the answer to these questions is "no," then keep searching for another subject. By the way, this is the best time to introduce yourself to the librarian. She may be able to tell you quickly whether or not your library has enough information on your subject.

• Ask yourself whether you can handle the topic within the space of your research paper. An eight- or nine-page paper isn't long enough to talk about the history of baseball, but is too long to stretch out a narrow topic such as the changing styles of baseball caps.

• Find out if your topic is acceptable to your teacher. Will the topic fulfill the requirements of the assignment? If your English teacher wants a biographical research paper, then one on famous haunted houses won't fill the bill.

If nothing strikes your fancy right away, here are a few tips to help you focus your thinking on a subject:

• Make a list of your interests and hobbies in order of importance to you. What kind of music do you listen to? What are your favorite school subjects? How do your spend your free time? What kinds of books and magazines do you read? What special skills or talents do you have? Look over your list and see if there are any related areas that have research paper possibilities.

• Just off the top of your head, complete these statements: "I would like to know more about . . . " or "I often wonder why . . . "

• If you weren't a student, what would you like to be doing instead?

• What is the biggest problem you think teenagers in your community face today?

• Ask your teacher to conduct a brainstorming session for the class. During brainstorming, each student, in turn, tosses out a writing idea which a recordkeeper writes on the blackboard. All ideas get an open forum and are not subject to criticism or comment when they are first listed. No idea is considered too far-fetched or unworkable at this point. After the class has exhausted its ideas, everyone then considers and discusses the merits of each one. At this stage, many ideas are rejected as unsuitable. The long list is honed down to a workable length, and a final pared-down list is made available to everyone in the class. To keep the brainstorming sessions under control, it helps to focus each session on a general subject such as popular culture, music, sports, and so on.

• Ask your teacher for guidance in selecting possible research-paper topics. After all, this may be your first attempt at writing a research paper. It helps to bounce ideas around with an expert who has probably read and corrected hundreds of such papers. Your teacher will have a pretty good idea of topics that worked for students in the past and those which are dead ends. You don't necessarily have to consult with the teacher who is assigning the paper, either. How about meeting with your music, gym, or art teacher to see if they have any ideas? They'll be flattered that you want to investigate some aspect of the subjects they teach, and since they're experts, they'll probably have good suggestions.

• Check the book listings (bibliographies) at the ends of chapters and at the back of your science, geography, or social studies textbooks. Most textbooks list dozens of subtopics related to the material covered in the book and provide you with a ready-made list of books on those subtopics. If you are studying the American Revolution, you may find a listing of books on what people were wearing at the time or what their houses were like during that period.

• Browse through a copy of *The Readers' Guide to Periodical Literature*. This is going to be one of your main sources for locating articles in magazines and newspapers. You'll find subject, title, and author entries in this guide. Why not thumb through some of the subject entries and see if anything appeals to you?

• Check out other reference books on the library shelves. The success of *The Book of Lists* and *The People's Almanac* has spawned a new generation of fact books, almanacs, encyclopedias, biographies, and dictionaries. While many of the references aren't meaty enough in themselves to use as primary reference sources, they are chock full of great ideas that might inspire an offbeat research paper. Here is a list of serious and not-so-serious references you might check for inspiration. You won't find every one of them in your library, but your librarian should be able to track down a few.

Fact Books:
The Book of Lists
Simon's List Book
Famous First Facts
Isaac Asimov's Book of Facts
Once Upon a Question
Encyclopedia of Amazing But True Facts
Almanac of Dates
Encyclopedia of Ignorance
Incomplete Book of Failures
Book of Numbers
Dictionary of Misinformation

Popular Culture References:

Curiosities of Popular Customs
Customs of Mankind
The Best, Worst, and Most Unusual
The Best of the Worst
Comic Book Heroes
The Film Encyclopedia
International Television Almanac
International Motion Picture Almanac
An Illustrated History of Horror Film
Dictionary of Costume
Book of Costume
Rock Encyclopedia
Grove's Dictionary of Music and Musicians
Encyclopedia of Popular Music in America
The Complete Encyclopedia of Popular Music
  and Jazz
Encyclopedia of Pop, Rock, and Jazz
The Complete Guide to Modern Dance
Dictionary of the Old West
The Encyclopedia of Food

Sports References:

Encyclopedia of Sports
Oxford Companion to World Sports and Games
The Baseball Encyclopedia: The Complete and
  Official Record of Major League Baseball
The Modern Encyclopedia of Basketball
The Official Encyclopedia of Football Games

Mystery References:

Encylopedia of Mystery and Detection
Detectionary
Who Done It?

14

Science Fiction and Fantasy:
Science Fiction Encyclopedia
A Dictionary of Fabulous Beasts
A Dictionary of Mythical Places
Science Fiction and Fantasy

Science:
Science in Everyday Life
Encyclopedia of Astronomy
Encyclopedia of Science and Technology
How Things Work
The New Space Encylopedia: A Guide to
  Astronomy and Space Exploration

Biography References:
People's Almanacs #1 and #2
People's Chronology
Very Special People

Hobby References:
World Stamps
World Air Power
Jane's All the World's Aircraft
Ships and Seafaring
Jane's Fighting Ships
World Stamps
Coins of the World
Catalogue of the World's Most Popular Coins
Encyclopedia of Chess
Complete Encyclopedia of Motorcars
Guinness Book of Car Facts

Language References
Dictionary of American Slang
Oddities and Curiosities of Words and Literature
Handy Book of Literary Curiosities
Dictionary of Bloopers and Boners
Dictionary of Word and Phrase Origins
New Dictionary of American Family Names
The Name Dictionary
American Nicknames, Their Origins, and
  Significance
Why Did They Name It?

Humor References:
Encyclopedia of Black Folklore and Humor
The Funniest Jokes and How to Tell Them
The Toastmaster's Treasure Chest
2,000 Insults for All Occasions
Throw a Tomato
20,000 Quips and Quotes

Folklore and the Supernatural:
Encyclopedia of Superstitions
Encyclopedia of the Unexplained: Magic,
  Occultism, and Parapsychology
The World's Most Famous Ghosts
Encyclopedia of Astrology
Encyclopedia of Mysticism, the Mystery Religions,
  and Occult Sciences
Superstitions, Folklore, and the Occult Sciences of
  the World

Oddities and Records:
Guinness Book of World Records
Amazing America
It's Against the Law

Catastrophe, Calamity, and Cataclysm
Guinness Book of Superstunts
Guinness Book of Superlatives
Ripley's Believe It or Not Book of Americana

Animal Reference Books:
Guinness Book of Animal Facts and Feats
Grzimek's Animal Life Encyclopedia
Mammals of the World
Animals of the Continents

• Finally, we've listed 150 possible research paper topics on page 93 of this book. Some may be too broad or narrow for your specific assignment, but they may trigger off more suitable variations of your own. Again, do a quick check of your library to see if there's enough information available on any of these topics. Then ask your teacher if he thinks the one you have picked is suitable for your assignment.

STEP 2: NARROW DOWN YOUR GENERAL SUBJECT AREA TO A SPECIFIC TOPIC

If this is your first research project, you may be wondering how on earth you're going to fill up all those assigned pages. Once you get going, though, you will discover, as many budding writers have before you, that your biggest job isn't expanding your topic but cutting it down to a workable size.

Imagine a tourist, camera in hand, faced with the Grand Canyon in front of him. While it's possible to get a vague, fuzzy image that looks something like the Grand Canyon into a snapshot, such a picture would probably be pretty dull. On the other hand, a photographer who focuses on a wildflower, tree branch, or small animal in the foreground will be more successful at conveying a sense of the canyon by just aiming at a piece of it. A carefully chosen detail, the well-thought-out angle or point of view, usually works much better than the broad overview. This applies to any effort—painting, picture taking, speaking, or writing.

With this in mind, you are ready to begin limiting your general writing subject. This is where an encyclopedia or some other general reference book is useful. The chapter or section on your general subject will suggest a number of subtopics, angles, questions, and viewpoints worth exploring. For example, suppose your general topic is: "Clothing Styles in the Last 100 Years." If you skim an encyclopedia section on the subject or browse through a general book on the history of clothing, you might discover these subtopics: teenage clothing fads; school dress codes; clothing styles as a political statement; the influence of military garb on fashions of the sixties; the adoption of work jeans as a fashion item; clothing styles that keep coming back. Any one of these narrower topics would be more suitable as a research paper subject than simply "Clothing Styles of the Last 100 Years."

Here are examples of a diagram that shows how a specific topic develops from a broad subject area. Each level represents a narrower version of the general subject.

Great Disasters

Manmade Disasters

Aviation Crashes

Mid-Air Collisions
in the Last Twenty
Years

United States Space Program

Projected Manned Space Flights

Current Astronaut Program

Future Careers in Outer Space

Endangered Animals

Animals Endangered in
International Waters

Cooperative Efforts of
Nations to Save
Endangered Animals

The Future of the
Blue Whale

Athletics
School Athletics
Government Regulations and School Sports
Changes in School-Athletics Funding as a Result of Recent Government Rulings

Music
Popular Music of the 1970s
Disco Music
The Effect of Disco Music on Fashion

Crime
Bank Robberies
Great Bank Heists of this Century

Trying It Out

Once you have decided on your general subject area, the next step is to develop it into a more focused topic.

Goal:

To narrow down your subject area to a topic suitable for your research paper.

Procedure:

1. After you have read over this chapter and picked a general subject area you like, list all the related topics you can find or think of.

_____   _____
_____   _____
_____   _____
_____   _____
_____   _____
_____   _____
_____   _____
_____   _____
_____   _____

2. Go over the narrowed-down topics on your list and check off those that seem like good possibilities.

3. Decide which topic of those you've checked you would most like to write about.

4. Ask yourself these questions:
  • Is my narrowed-down topic acceptable to the teacher?
  • Is there enough available research material on this topic in my library?
  • Is the topic too personal? Will I have to depend too heavily on my own experiences, opinions, and feelings?

5. While your preliminary research for a narrowed topic is still fresh in your mind, list all the reactions, ideas, and questions you have about the topic. Include everything that pops into your head; you will hone down this list later on.

_____
_____
_____
_____
_____
_____
_____
_____
_____

STEP 3: WRITE A THESIS STATEMENT

Let's suppose you have found a general subject you like, say, hockey. After some quick browsing through the card catalog, an encyclopedia on sports, and *The Readers' Guide to Periodical Literature*, you come up with these subtopics: Players' Salaries in the NHL, The History of the Stanley Cup, or Common Injuries in Professional Hockey. You decide to write about players' salaries because you are interested in the subject and have read a lot about it in the last year. You have checked out the topic with your teacher, and she gives you the go-ahead. What happens next?

To make your paper personal and meaningful, the next step is to form some kind of opinion about your topic. A statement of your opinion or main idea is called your *thesis statement*.

A thesis statement is a sentence or two which indicates the approach you plan to take with your topic. It is a summary of your goals, your aims, and the main idea of your research paper. All your later research must tie in with your thesis statement. You'll even find that the way you decide to organize your paper will be related to the kind of thesis statement you make.

Let's take a look at some examples of thesis statements based on various research topics:

Topics	Thesis Statement
Irish Migration in the Late Nineteenth and Early Twentieth Centuries	The Great Potato Famine, combined with the restrictive policies of the English government, drove millions of Irish from their country during the mid- to late 1800s and the early 1900s.
Factors That Influenced Fashion in the Last Two Decades	Clothing styles used to filter down from the rich to the middle and lower classes. However, in the late 1960s, clothing styles such as ethnic costumes; military garb; and working class denims, work shirts, and work and cowboy boots were picked up by designers who created clothes for the upper classes.

Bicycle Safety	The rising number of bike-related accidents can be prevented in a number of ways.
Robots in Everyday Life	Robots are not only found in the latest science-fiction movies, but in countless offices and schools.
Courtship Customs Among American Teenagers in the Last 100 Years	One-to-one boy-girl dating is a fairly recent development in the social lives of teenagers.
The History of Common Superstitions	Many current superstitions have their roots in folklore and witch-craft.

Your thesis statement is a decision to follow a certain direction in your research. This declaration determines the organization of your outline and the kinds of research materials you will use. The thesis statement helps you and your reader follow a train of thought throughout your paper.

Here are several points to keep in mind when you prepare your thesis statement:

• Write your statement in a declarative sentence. Avoid putting your thesis statement in a question, phrase, or word.

• Write a thesis statement that is somewhat open to argument, debate, or speculation. Your reader will then want to read on to see how you prove your point with facts, data, and well-formed opinions.

• Make sure your thesis statement covers only what you plan to discuss in your paper.

Trying It Out

Goal:

To form a thesis statement for your paper, based on the ideas you've gathered.

Procedure:

1. Look over the list of ideas you've written down so far. Find at least five or six of them that seem to tie together and write them down.

_____   _____
_____   _____
_____   _____
_____   _____
_____

2. Check off the two most interesting ideas on your list.

3. Look over this list. Think of one main idea that pulls the two most interesting ideas together.

4. Write down your main idea in the form of a declarative sentence or two. This is your thesis statement.

5. Make sure your thesis statement clearly indicates your topic and the plan you have for handling the topic in your paper.

Progress Check

Fill in the blanks below to see how well your paper is progressing at this stage. If you discover any problem areas, see what you can do about them. Perhaps just a quick meeting with your teacher will help you get over any hurdles you encounter.

Topic: _____

Thesis statement: _____

Where I am so far:
_____ have only read this chapter
_____ have done preliminary research to find a general subject
_____ have narrowed down the general subject to a specific topic
_____ have listed all my ideas, reactions, and questions about my topic
_____ have pulled together selected ideas from my list into a thesis statement

Problems I'm having:
_____ finding a general subject
_____ narrowing down a general subject to a specific topic
_____ finding materials in the library
_____ making a list of ideas about my narrowed-down topic
_____ writing a thesis statement
_____ other_____

_____

Chapter 2

DOWN TO BASICS: Researching and Notetaking

Planning your research is a little like shopping in a large supermarket: The job is a lot easier if you have a good idea of what you want ahead of time, arrive with a list in hand, and know the layout of the place you are going to. The research portion of your project will move along quickly if you've formulated the main idea of your paper, gathered a few preliminary notes, and become acquainted with your library.

STEP 4: GATHER INFORMATION IN THE LIBRARY

Before you begin digging into the actual research sources for your paper, there are a few things you can do at home to prepare for your library work. Here are some tips to consider before you set out:

• Decide whether interviewing or surveying people is a good starting point for your research. You may want to postpone your library visit until your surveys are complete. That way you'll be able to look for sources that back up the results of your interviews or surveys.

• Look over any preliminary notes you've made about your subject so far. Study your thesis statement. What kinds of books and references are most likely to support your point of view? Should you be checking facts? Then almanacs, yearbooks, and atlases will be a big help. Do you think the opinions of experts will help you argue or prove the main point of your paper? Then you'll need magazine and newspaper articles, journals, or perhaps primary sources like biographies, autobiographies, and diaries. Is your paper going to be about past events or historical figures? Then you'll be heading for the historical or biographical shelves of the library.

• Bring the following materials to the library: your library card, pens and pencils, index cards for notetaking, and this book to help you find your way through all those library materials.

Checking Out the Library

Even a school library can seem confusing when you are trying to track down information on just one subject. Those aisles and shelves of books can look pretty overwhelming if all you need to find out is Babe Ruth's batting average in a particular year. Fortunately, nearly all libraries are organized according to a logical system which you can master in less than half an hour. Ask the librarian for a brief guided tour. That way you won't spend valuable time wandering around aimlessly searching for what you need.

Trying It Out

You'll be spending several hours in the library during the coming weeks. Familiarize yourself with the facilities and services it offers by completing the steps below.

Goal:

To learn how to use the library.

Procedure:

1. Obtain a printed floor plan of your library if one is available. If not, draw up your own floor plan or write down the exact location of the following resources:

- circulation desk
- card catalog
- indexes for periodicals, magazines, and newspapers
- bound volumes of periodicals, magazines, and newspapers
- current periodicals, magazines, and newspapers
- general reference shelves
- fiction shelves
- non-fiction shelves
- biography shelves
- vertical files (file cabinets of clippings, pamphlets, maps, pictures, etc.)

- audio-visual materials and equipment (filmstrips, records, cassettes, microfilm, etc.)
- reading room or area

2. Find out the rules of your particular library from the librarian. Then answer these questions:

- Do you give the librarian a call slip to gain access to materials, or can you remove materials from the shelves yourself?
- Do you follow the same procedure for gaining access to all types of materials—periodicals, records, books, vertical file materials? _____
- Which materials can be taken out of the building and which must be used in the building?_____
- Is there any limit to the quantity of materials you can check out?_____
- How do you check out materials? Go about returning them? _____

The Card Catalog

Libraries keep track of the materials they store by filing a small information card on every book they receive. These cards are then stored in the card catalog, a cabinet of small drawers in a central location where you can easily check them. The drawers are alphabetically arranged as are the file cards inside them.

The card catalog is a master file of every book the library owns. (Some libraries list cards for records and filmstrips in the card catalog as well.) The card catalog tells you whether a particular title, author, or subject is represented by some book in the library. It provides the convenience of listing more than one card for each book. You can find a non-fiction book listed on three different types of cards: an author card, a title card, or a subject card. Books of fiction are listed on two kinds of cards: a title card and an author card.

Subject Cards: When you first begin your research, the only information you may have is the subject you're investigating. If you want to find out just what materials your library has on it, look up your subject—say, "Cars"—under that heading to see what is available. Libraries sometimes use different labels for a subject, so if you don't find a card on the first try, think of other headings your subject might come under. In this case, "Automobiles" or "Motor Vehicles" might be alternate headings. The card catalog often breaks down a subject into subtopics. You might find cards for "Cars–racing" or "Cars–technology." Consider using these subtopics when you get around to narrowing down your general subject.

Title Cards: Perhaps all you have is a book title you want to check. Look under the first main word of the title to find the card. Here are some filing rules to follow when you flip through title cards:

• *A*, *An*, and *The* are not counted as part of the title, and the card is filed alphabetically under the next word.

• Titles that begin with abbreviations or numbers are filed as though the words were actually spelled out. You would look for *Dr.* as though it were written out as *Doctor*. *U.S.* in a title would be filed under *United States*.

• Numerals in a title are filed as though they were spelled out in words. *101 Gifts to Make and Give* would be filed as *One Hundred and One Gifts to Make and Give*.

• *Mc* names are filed as though they were spelled *Mac*. *McKenzie*, for example, is filed as *MacKenzie*.

Author Cards: If you know the author of the book you're looking for, check the last name in the card catalog. Cards for authors with the same last name are first filed by the last name, then alphabetically by the first name; for example, Ryan, Cornelius would be filed before Ryan, Elizabeth. When the library has several books by the same author, the cards are filed by the last name, then alphabetically by the title of each book.

The card catalog does more than just tell you whether or not a particular book or author is represented on the library's shelves. These cards often list the kind of information you'll find in a particular book, such as:

• publication dates; name and country of publisher; subsequent printings of the book. This information tells you how current the material is.

• charts, maps, graphs, or special illustrations. This may come in handy if you need visual information to back up your research.

• the number of pages in the book.

• whether the book contains a bibliography. This can be a big help if you are looking for other books related to your subject.

• a summary of what the book is about. This summary can help you decide whether the book will be useful in your research or not.

When it comes time to prepare bibliography cards, you can get all the necessary information directly from the card catalog without having to pull the book itself from the shelves.

On pages 34–36 are sample title, author, and subject cards for a biography anthology called *Lift Every Voice* by Dorothy Sterling.

920
S

Lift Every Voice
Sterling, Dorothy, 1913–
    Lift every voice; the lives of Booker T. Washington,
W. E. B. Du Bois, Mary Church Terrell, and James Weldon Johnson [by] Dorothy Sterling and Benjamin Quarles.
Illustrated by Ernest Crichlow. [1st ed.] Garden City,
N. Y., Doubleday, 1965.
    116 p. illus., ports. 22 cm. (Zenith books)
    Short biographies of four Negro leaders whose beliefs and achievements are important in the history of American Negroes.

    1. Washington, Booker, Tallaferro, 1859–1915. 2. Du Bois, William Edward Burghardt, 1868–1963. 3. Terrell, Mary (Church) 1863–1954. 4. Johnson, James Weldon, 1871–1938. I. Quarles, Benjamin, joint author. II. Crichlow, Ernest, 1914– illus. III. Title.

E185.96.S77   920   A C 66–6569

Library of Congress   [1]

920
S

Sterling, Dorothy, 1913–
 Lift every voice; the lives of Booker T. Washington, W. E. B. Du Bois, Mary Church Terrell, and James Weldon Johnson ₍by₎ Dorothy Sterling and Benjamin Quarles. Illustrated by Ernest Crichlow. ₍1st ed.₎ Garden City, N. Y., Doubleday, 1965.

 116 p. illus., ports. 22 cm. (Zenith books)

 Short biographies of four Negro leaders whose beliefs and achievements are important in the history of American Negroes.

 1. Washington, Booker, Taliaferro, 1859–1915. 2. Du Bois, William Edward Burghardt, 1868–1963. 3. Terrell, Mary (Church) 1863–1954. 4. Johnson, James Weldon, 1871–1938. I. Quarles, Benjamin, joint author. II. Crichlow, Ernest, 1914– illus. III. Title.

E185.96.S77   920   A C 66–6569

920
S

WASHINGTON, BOOKER, TALIAFERRO, 1859–1915.

Sterling, Dorothy, 1913–

Lift every voice; the lives of Booker T. Washington, W. E. B. Du Bois, Mary Church Terrell, and James Weldon Johnson [by] Dorothy Sterling and Benjamin Quarles. Illustrated by Ernest Crichlow. [1st ed.] Garden City, N. Y., Doubleday, 1965.

116 p. illus., ports. 22 cm. (Zenith books)

Short biographies of four Negro leaders whose beliefs and achievements are important in the history of American Negroes.

1. Washington, Booker, Taliaferro, 1859–1915. 2. Du Bois, William Edward Burghardt, 1868–1963. 3. Terrell, Mary (Church) 1863–1954. 4. Johnson, James Weldon, 1871–1938. I. Quarles, Benjamin, joint author. II. Crichlow, Ernest, 1914– illus. III. Title.

E185.96.S77   920   A C 66–6569

Library of Congress   [1]

Call Numbers

The cards in the card catalog have one other important piece of information on them—*call numbers*. These letter and number codes appear in the upper left-hand corner of each card and correspond to a matching code on the spine of the book. The call number is, in fact, a kind of address code that tells you where each book is located on the shelves.

When you want the librarian to pull a book from the closed shelves, you write down the call number, title, and author on a *call slip*. These are small printed pieces of paper which you fill out. If you are allowed to go to the shelves and pull books yourself, the information you record on the call slip will help you find the book more quickly.

Fiction: Novels are classified as fiction and are shelved in a special section. They are arranged in alphabetical order by the author's last name. The call number for a novel is usually a combination of letters. For example, the call number for a novel by Ernest Hemingway might appear as H or Hem. The top line tells you the book is in the fiction section, and the bottom line gives you the first letter(s) of the author's last name.

Biographies: Books in the biography collection of your library are listed not by author but by the last name of the person written about in the book. If the book is about one person, the call number on the top line is either 92, which stands for *biography* in the Dewey Decimal System, or *B* for biography. The letter or letters that follow indicate the first letter(s) of the subject's last name.

Example: $\dfrac{92}{W}$ or $\dfrac{92}{Wa}$ or $\dfrac{B}{Wash}$

for books about George Washington

Biography collections about several people are listed in the card catalog and on the shelves by the author who compiled the collection. These group biographies are located on the shelves immediately after the single-biography books.

Non-Fiction:
The Dewey Decimal System

This call number system makes it possible for librarians to group all non-fiction books into the following main categories:

- 000-099   General works: reference books
- 100-199   Philosophy and Psychology
- 200-299   Religion and Mythology
- 300-399   Social Sciences (customs, laws, educational methods, occupations, etc.)
- 400-499   Languages (linguistics, foreign languages, and dictionaries)
- 500-599   Pure Science (mathematics, chemistry, biology, etc.)
- 600-699   Technology (medicine, aviation, engineering, home economics, etc.)
- 700-799   Fine Arts; Recreation (architecture, painting, sports, music, dancing, hobbies, etc.)
- 800-899   Literature (poetry, plays, essays, criticism, speeches, letters, etc.)

- 900-999 History (geography, travel, biography, ancient and modern history)

Numbers that fall after the decimal point give
more information about the book. Here are a few
rules to keep in mind about the arrangement of
non-fiction books in most libraries:

- Non-fiction books are shelved from left to
right. The lower-numbered books begin on the
left. As you go right, the numbers get higher.

- The first letter of the author's last name appears under each number of a non-fiction book.

- Books are filed in numerical order. If several
non-fiction books share the same number, they
are then arranged alphabetically by the initial of
the author's last name.

Trying It Out

Goal:
To use the card catalog to locate at least
one book for your research paper.

Procedure:
1. Find one subject card, one author
card, and one title card in the card catalog,
for a book related to your research topic.

2. Complete a call slip to retrieve the
book from the shelves.

Indexes

Reference books—books of information that
must only be used in the library—fall into two
general categories. Encyclopedias, yearbooks,

almanacs, and atlases—all one type—contain data about thousands of subjects. They are discussed in the next section. The other type of reference book, the index, is a *listing* of magazine and newspaper articles that have been written about a particular subject.

Just as the card catalog is a master listing of books, an index is a master listing of periodical articles that have been published. Similarly, entries in an index are arranged by subject and author (title entries are limited to short stories and plays). You can sit down with a single volume of a periodical index and locate the title, author, date, and subject of every major magazine article written during a particular year. This saves you the effort of thumbing through scores of magazines, searching for information.

The Readers' Guide to Periodical Literature Index:

The main index you'll be using for your research paper is *The Readers' Guide to Periodical Literature* index. It lists articles published in American magazines since 1900. Each volume is arranged by year. If you are researching a very current topic, your best bet is to check the most recent volumes and work your way back. Otherwise, check volumes for the years you plan to cover in your research.

To save on space, the *Readers' Guide* uses many abbreviations. These are clearly explained in the front of each volume. To use the *Readers' Guide*, look up the most important or key word in your subject. If the index doesn't happen to use that particular heading, you'll probably find a cross reference telling you exactly what subject heading to check elsewhere in the index. If you are checking information about movies or plays—perhaps reviews—you would probably find information under their individual titles and under categories like "Moving Pictures" or "Drama." Under a person's name, you would find two kinds of entries. One type lists any articles by the person; a second entry lists articles about that person.

Here is a sample page from the *Readers' Guide* on the subject of alcohol.

New process makes gasoline from alcohol. E.
Smay. il Pop Sci 212:90-1 Je '78
Progress on alcohol fuels. J. Schinto. Progres-
sive 42:12-13 Jl '78
Tankful of sugar; program in Brazil. R. C.
Schroeder. Américas 31:19-20 Ja '78
We've been asked: about using alcohol as a
fuel for automobiles. il U.S. News 84:51 Ja 16
'78
ALCOHOL, Drug Abuse and Mental Health Ad-
ministration. See United States—Alcohol.
Drug Abuse and Mental Health Administra-
tion
ALCOHOL education. See Temperance—Study
and teaching
ALCOHOL, Tobacco and Firearms, Bureau of.
See United States—Alcohol, Tobacco and Fire-
arms, Bureau of
ALCOHOLIC beverages
Cost-effective: fortifying alcoholic beverages
with thiamine to forestall Wernicke-Korsa-
koff syndrome. Sci Am 239:90+ O '78
Cozy drinks to keep you warm when the
weather's not. A. Fraser. Mademoiselle 84:236
O '78
Fluid forms of fauna and flora: recipes. H.
McNulty. il House & Gard 150:208+ N '78
Holiday cheer: gifts for everyone on your list.
A. Fraser. Mademoiselle 84:86 D '78
How to be your own bartender. il Glamour
76:226 D '78
How to give the summer's best—and cheapest
—party. il Mademoiselle 84:180-1+ Je '78
Serving tips for holiday drinks. Good H 187:
317 D '78
Summer coolers. J. White. il Essence 9:97+ Jl
'78
10 new thirst quenchers to serve at a summer
party. il Glamour 76:242 Je '78
Toasting Christmas. H. McNulty. por House &
Gard 150:142 D '78
See also
Beer
Cocktails
Liquors
Punch (beverage)
Wine

Labeling

Agency drags its feet on warning to pregnant
women. R. J. Smith. Science 199:748-9 F 17 '78
Caution: too many health warnings could be
counterproductive: study of proposed labeling
of alcoholic beverages by BAFT. A. Etzioni.
il Psychol Today 12:20+ D '78

ALCOHOLICS
Sickness in the family. J. Allen and S. C. Hart-
man. McCalls 106:95+ O '78
See also
Alcohol and authors
Alcohol and automobile drivers
Alcohol and women
Alcohol and youth
Children of alcoholics
Church work with alcoholics

Rehabilitation

See Alcoholism—Therapy
ALCOHOLICS Anonymous
Second Chance: guest house for alcoholics. S.
Hart. il Blair & Ketchums 5:74-83 D '78
See also
Al-Anon Family Group, Inc
ALCOHOLISM
Alcoholism in marriage: some causes and cures.
C. Deutsch. por Parents Mag 53:38 D '78
Drinking as a way of life: liquor problem in
Japan. il Time 111:58 My 22 '78
Dual addiction: alcohol and drugs. W. Stock-
ton. il N Y Times Mag p 10-11+ Ag 6 '78
Impact of alcohol on health and society. H. K.
Panjwani. Consumers Res Mag 61:12-14 F '78
See also
Alcohol—Physiological effects
Alcohol and authors
Alcohol and automobile drivers
Alcohol and women
Alcohol and youth
Alcoholics
Delirium tremens
Liquor problem
United States—National Institute of Alcohol
Abuse and Alcoholism

Trying It Out

Goal:

To find at least two articles mentioned in the *Readers' Guide*, related to your research paper.

Procedure:

1. Go to the *Readers' Guide* and pull out a volume for the time period you are researching.

2. Look up a main topic or a subtopic you would like to research for your paper.

3. When you locate a promising entry, write down the following information on a call slip so that the librarian can pull the magazine for you: name of magazine, date of issue, volume, title of article (in quotation marks), author's name, and the pages where the article appears.

General References

There are times when neither books nor magazine articles on your subject answer specific questions you have or give you a broad enough overview. Reference books collect information on thousands of subjects which would take you forever to track down if you had to search for them individually in books, magazines, and newspapers. General references boil down information and arrange it so that a researcher can find it quickly. Since reference books are designed for fast consultation, they can only be used in the library. Familiarizing yourself with the books on the general reference shelves gives you a big jump on your research.

Here are the most likely references you will come across in an average-sized library:

Encyclopedias: These multi-volume collections offer brief general information on persons, places, and branches of knowledge. They are invaluable in giving you a broad overview of your general subject early in your research. Articles in them may suggest a number of subtopics you'll want to explore. Since they are written to provide an overview of a subject, you should not rely on them as the primary sources for your research. They should be used early on as a guide to the subtopics you plan to pursue more specifically elsewhere. **Examples:** *Compton's* and *World Book Encyclopedia* are suitable for most high school research papers. More advanced are: *Encyclopedia Brittanica* and *Collier's Encyclopedia*. **How to use:** Check the alphabetical index at the back of the encyclopedia. The index lists all the subjects included in the collection. Some sets have the index for the entire collection in one volume; others include an index in each volume. The index is particularly helpful when you are researching a broad topic and not all the information about it is in one encyclopedia article.

Yearbooks and Almanacs: These fact books are published yearly and contain short articles and listings of special events that took place in a given year. Most encyclopedias also publish single-volume yearbooks describing current events of that year. These are helpful when you want the most up-to-date information about a general topic. Each yearbook has its own index.

Almanacs provide facts and figures on countries, sports, celebrities, events like the Olympics or a political convention, and much more. **Examples:** *The World Almanac*, *Information Please*, *Facts on File* (updated weekly in larger libraries). **How to use:** Look up your subject in the index, then scan the list of subtopics to find the exact fact you are investigating.

Biographical dictionaries: These summaries of famous people's lives can tell you a celebrity's hobbies, marital status, educational background, nicknames, accomplishments, and more. While you would read a general biography of someone you were writing a paper about, biographical dictionaries offer useful and fascinating tidbits in condensed form. These items can add a special flavor to your paper. **Examples:** *Who's Who in America*, *Webster's Biographical Dictionary*, *Current Biography*, *Contemporary Authors*. For deceased figures: *The New York Times Obituary Index*, *Dictionary of American Biography*, *Who Was Who in America*, *Dictionary of National Biography*. **How to use:** Simply look up the last name of the person you are researching.

Maps, Atlases, Gazeteers: These geographical references contain maps of countries plus charts and facts about the world, its peoples, and resources. **Examples:** *Rand McNally*, *Hammond's*, *Goode's School Atlas*. **How to use:** Look up the name of the country, city, or continent in the index or alphabetical listing.

STEP 5: TAKE NOTES ON INDEX CARDS

The key to a well-developed research paper is a collection of comprehensive, clearly written notes. Your notes determine the course your paper will take. They support your thesis statement, personal opinions, and generalizations. The organization of your notes paves the way for your outline and the method of development you will follow in your paper. Just from a practical standpoint, complete notes written down during a couple of library sessions will mean you won't have to have your research sources on hand when you get to the writing part of your project. Nor should you have to return to your sources a second time if you take thorough notes in the first place.

The format for doing this is a set of bibliography cards you prepare citing all the outside sources you've researched. You may be wondering why you can't simply copy your sources and notes on regular notebook paper. Actually, you can if your teacher allows you to. Over the years, however, professional researchers have developed a more flexible and efficient tool for gathering and recording notes—the index card.

Index cards—one per source—enable you to arrange your reference sources in alphabetical order for your final bibliography sheet. Second, when you write out actual notes on an index note card—one idea per card—you can later arrange the cards in related groupings, shuffle them around, or discard those you don't plan to use. When you're ready to do your outline, you then arrange the cards in the sequence you plan to follow. This card system also gives you the advantage of feeding more cards into your collection without rearranging the whole system. Sheets of notebook paper would not allow you this flexibility of selecting, recording, and arranging your notes. You would wind up with arrows, deletion marks, and additions going in every direction. So a pack of a hundred cards or so is an investment in your time, energy, and efficiency. Consider using them even if they aren't a requirement of the assignment.

Bibliography Cards

A working bibliography is a set of cards you compile for your own use when you begin your library research. This bibliography lists every book, article, or reference that provides background or information for your paper. You can obtain the information for these cards from the card catalog, *Readers' Guide*, or directly from the materials themselves. A complete set of cards in your working bibliography will save you from backtracking when you pull together your final footnotes and bibliography sheet. If it turns out that you don't use a particular source after all, simply throw out the card.

The following information is included in a bibliography card for a book:
1. author's name, last name first
2. book title, underlined
3. where published
4. publisher's name
5. year book was published

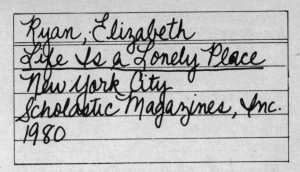

Ryan, Elizabeth
Life Is a Lonely Place
New York City
Scholastic Magazines, Inc.
1980

You can locate all this information on the title or copyright page of the book or from a matching card in the card catalog.

The following information is included in a bibliography card for a magazine article:

1. author's name, last name first
2. title of article, in quotation marks
3. name of magazine or periodical, underlined
4. volume number
5. date of periodical
6. exact pages on which article appears

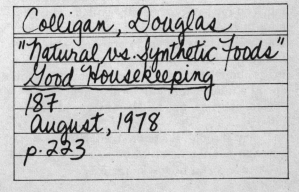

Colligan, Douglas
"Natural vs. Synthetic Foods"
Good Housekeeping
187
August, 1978
p. 223

An encyclopedia bibliography card includes the following information:

1. name of encyclopedia
2. author's name, if signed
3. topic, in quotation marks
4. year of edition
5. volume
6. page of article

World Book Encyclopedia
Shoemaker, Eugene M.
"Moon"
1979
13
pp. 646-651

With your bibliography cards in hand, you are ready to pull books, magazines, and references from the shelves and begin your actual notetaking. You can save yourself the bother of lugging a lot of books home if you learn how to skim your research materials. In any case, you have to use general references and periodicals right in the library anyway, so skimming can help you spend a minimal amount of time there.

Here are some tips for skimming reading material:

1. Flip through the entire book from cover to cover to get a general impression of what the book covers and how it's organized.

2. Read the Foreword or Preface to find out the author's purpose and point of view. Does his or her statement coincide with your thesis statement?

3. Read over the table of contents to get an overview of the book. If you find an entry related to your topic, turn to that section and take notes from it.

4. Pay attention to the chapter headings, subheadings, and words in bold type.

5. Take note of charts, graphs, diagrams, and other visuals.

In the case of periodical articles, do a fast run-through of the material to see if there's anything usable there. Be especially alert to opening paragraphs, where writers usually state their most important points.

Note Cards

Your set of bibliography cards is one part of your notetaking system; your note cards are another. On them you will record all the factual information you research for your paper. Good notes are a real timesaver; you won't have to return to your sources again if you take thorough notes from the beginning.

Start reading the sources that seemed most promising when you selected your research materials. You should be looking for an author's main ideas, supporting examples, data, and conclusions. Be alert for quotations that back up your own thesis statement or other main ideas you have. Keep in mind that the purpose of your notetaking isn't to summarize entire books or articles but simply to get specific information that relates to various points you plan to make in your paper.

Here are a few tips to set up your notetaking system on index cards:

1. **Think of a heading that summarizes the kind of information you are recording.** Write that heading in the top left-hand corner of the index card above the information itself. These headings will later become entries on your outline. For the topic, "Coincidences," you might have note-card headings like: "Coincidences Involving Dreams," "Animal Coincidences," "Coincidences Involving Luck or Curses." You can use headings more than once; in fact, if you only have one card for a particular category, you probably won't be able to develop it in enough detail in your paper.

2. **Make sure you write down the name of the source (title or author's last name) and the page numbers** showing exactly where the information is located in the source. Write this information in the upper right-hand corner of the card. Nothing is more frustrating than getting to the writing stage and discovering that you don't have a page number for your footnote.

3. **Record only one kind of information per card** even if it's from the same book. Later on you will be grouping the cards by headings, and you'll run into problems sorting out the cards if you have different types of information on a single card.

4. **Write only on one side of the card.** You've probably invested in a large pack of note cards—don't skimp on them.

5. **Avoid writing out complete sentences** *ex-*

cept in the case of direct quotations or passages you want to excerpt.

6. **There are several types of note cards you can write:**

• a paraphrase in which you put another person's ideas into your own words.

• a direct quotation which you copy word for word from your source.

• a summary which condenses a great deal of material into a short amount of space.

• a short outline in which you describe the information in terms of main and supporting ideas.

Here are some sample note cards:

Coincidences, Dreams   Colligan, p.74

Psychologist David Ryback says that some dreams predicting exact future events do come true.

One subject dreamed he was a witness to a bank robbery, and the night after the dream, he did witness a bank robbery in the exact bank he had dreamed about.

<u>Coincidences, Animals</u> Colligan
pp. 62-63

One family's cat, Daisy,
found her way back, 600
miles, to New York City,
after having been aban-
doned in an upstate
town.

Trying It Out

Goal:

To write note cards on all the research
materials you have gathered for your
paper.

Procedure:

1. Write a note card for every piece of
information you locate that you think will
be useful in your paper. When in doubt,
write it out. It's easier to throw out an un-
used card later on than have to go back to
a source you forgot to record.

2. Make sure you have a heading in the
top left-hand corner that describes the kind
of information you wrote down.

3. Check that you have included the
name of the source (title or author) and the
exact page numbers where the information
appears.

4. Double-check that all quotations and excerpted passages are recorded word for word as they appear in the original source.

Progress Check

Fill in the blanks below to see how well your paper is progressing at this point. Check with your teacher about any problems you are encountering.

Where I am so far:
_____ have been to the library
_____ have started research
_____ have written up all the bibliography cards
_____ have written up all the note cards

Problems I'm having:
_____ using the library
_____ finding enough sources
_____ taking concise notes
_____ other: _____

Chapter 3

WRITE ON: The Outline and First Draft

Let's assume you've been diligently following the suggested steps in this book for preparing a research paper. You decided on a general subject you liked. You narrowed it down to a manageable size. You invested in note cards and arrived at the library with a pack of them in hand. After following the advice in this book, you are almost on a first-name basis with the librarian and can practically find your way around the library in the dark. You have written down bibliography cards, tracked down books, articles, and reference information related to your topic, and duly noted all this information on those index cards.

Now you have a small pile of bibliography

cards and a larger pile of perhaps thirty or more note cards. You check your calendar and realize you only have eleven more days before your research paper is due. Panic sets in. You've been doing what seem like odds and ends for the last few weeks and what do you have to show for it? A topic, a thesis statement, a pile of cards, and a headful of jumbled information. At this point, you're probably wondering just exactly how all these bits and pieces are going to transform themselves into a well-written research paper.

Well, you can relax a little. Believe it or not, you've done over half the work already, and the most difficult half, at that. You now have nearly all the raw materials you'll need for your paper. Most of the library work is complete. If you have taken good notes, you probably won't even have to go back to the library again. Your next step is to pull together your note cards and use them as a basis for an outline. Your outline will be a blueprint for the rest of your paper. When it is in order, you will begin the actual writing of your paper.

ARRANGING YOUR NOTE CARDS

When you took notes on your index cards, you wrote a heading in the upper left-hand corner of each card. In a word or two, this heading described the type of research information you wrote on that card. For example, note cards for a research paper on the gasoline crunch might have note cards with these headings in the corner:

- problems caused by gas shortage
- effect on driving habits
- effect on automobile buying habits
- causes of shortage
- proposed solutions

Your own note-card headings will now help you pull your notes into a working plan for your paper.

Trying It Out

Goal:
To arrange your note cards in related groups.

Procedure:
1. Flip through all your note cards.
2. Group cards with the same headings.
3. See if there are any "strays," that is, single cards which don't fit into any group. If any of these cards seem worthwhile, you may have to go back to the library to find one or two other related pieces of information for that category. A single card doesn't really provide enough supporting information for a main idea. If the information on the extra card seems unlikely to fit into your unfolding work plan, then discard it.
4. Once your cards are grouped, you should examine each grouping to see if you have enough supporting material to back up your thesis and main ideas in your pa-

per. If certain groups seem skimpy, then plan one more library visit to fill in the gaps with more information.

GROUPING YOUR NOTE CARDS BY ORGANIZATIONAL PATTERNS

Once you have categorized your cards, eliminated those you can't use, and filled in any gaps with newly researched cards, you need to choose a logical arrangement for your pieces of information. Here are some of the most common methods for organizing and developing a research paper:

1. **Analysis.** Using this pattern, you show how something works. An example of a thesis statement that could be developed by analysis: Communications satellites have changed the way television programs are being broadcast.

2. **Chronology.** This method develops a topic according to time sequence. The chronological pattern works well with research papers that trace the development of historical events or trends. Example: The immigration laws of the last fifty years have affected the ethnic composition of many big-city neighborhoods.

3. **Comparison/Contrast.** With this method, you take two or more aspects of a topic and show their similarities and differences. This is an especially effective method to follow when you

want to show differing sides of an issue or indicate preference for one thing over another. Example: Rock-and-roll is a corrupt form of rhythm-and-blues.

4. **Problem/Solution.** This is a useful pattern to consider if you raise a problem in your thesis statement and plan to show the solutions to the problem in the body of your paper. Example: Crowded traffic conditions in our major cities have reached alarming proportions and are adversely affecting the quality of city life.

5. **Topical.** With this method you break down your topic into smaller ones. Example: Television viewing has had a powerful effect on the way families spend time together; on the reading habits of children; and on the buying habits of consumers.

6. **Opinion/Reasons.** Using this technique, you state your opinion about your topic then give reasons, based on your research, for holding that opinion. Example: Motorcycle helmet laws should be mandatory in every state.

The organizational pattern you choose should be flexible. You may even want to combine several of the above methods to develop your thesis statement. In any case, it is important to have a clear idea of how to organize your information before you get to the actual writing of your first draft.

Trying It Out

Now that you have organized your note cards, you are ready to consider possible ways of organizing that material.

Goal:

To choose a suitable method or methods of organization for developing your thesis statement.

Procedure:

1. Write down your thesis statement.

_____

_____

2. Look over your note-card groupings and study the kind of supporting information you have gathered. Which organizational pattern would work best for the kind of information you have on your cards?_____

_____

_____

3. In a sentence or two, state why your chosen organizational method(s) especially suit(s) your topic and the research you have done. _____

_____

_____

STEP 6: WRITE UP AN OUTLINE BASED ON YOUR NOTE CARDS

All this shuffling of cards and decision-making about the organization of your paper leads up to the key to your paper—the outline. While you may have heard of students who, to satisfy a requirement of the assignment, manufactured an outline after writing their papers, there are a number of excellent reasons other than an assignment requirement for working from an outline.

An outline is the bare-bones skeleton of your paper. It presents your plan in an organized way, points out gaps in your research, and keeps you on the track. Students who work without one, or slap together something after the fact, create a lot of extra work for themselves. It's a lot easier to add or delete an entry in an outline than to write or omit entire paragraphs from several pages of an actual paper. Writing without an outline is like setting out on a long trip to a new place without a road map. It's possible to get to the destination, but it will take a lot longer than if you had checked a map in the first place.

The work you have completed so far in labeling and grouping your note cards is the basis for your outline. Once you have categorized your note cards, those headings in the corner become the main ideas in the outline. The research information on the cards becomes the supporting details of these main headings. The sequence of your outline will be the organizational method you chose for arranging your card groups.

Here is the customary outline format for a research paper. Depending on the number of note cards you have, however, your own outline may have more or fewer entries than the number shown here.

Model Outline

Your Name: _____
Date: _____
Course: _____
Teacher: _____

Thesis Statement: _____

Introduction: Opening sentences. Thesis statement. (Many writers work on the introduction after the body of the paper is finished.)

Development:

I. First Main Idea (The heading for this entry comes from the heading on the first group of note cards you plan to use in your paper.)
  A. Supporting Idea (Use information from your note cards in as many sentences as you need to develop the main idea.)
    1. Further supporting ideas or information
    2.
    3.
  B. Supporting Idea
    1.
    2.
    3.
  C. Supporting Idea
    1.
    2.
    3.

II. Second Main Idea (Use the same heading as the category heading on your second group of note cards.)
   A. Supporting Idea
      1.
      2.
   B. Supporting Idea
   C. Supporting Idea
   D. Supporting Idea
III. Continue following this number and letter pattern until you have listed all the headings, supporting ideas, and information from each pack of cards.

Conclusion: Review your thesis statement. Summarize the main ideas you have presented. Give your conclusions. (In the outline, you can state this information in a few sentences which you will polish up in your drafts.)

Trying It Out

Goal:

To produce an outline for your research paper.

Procedure:

1. Lay out your card groupings in front of you. Choose the first group and write the heading from those cards next to the first Roman numeral entry in the form below.

2. Keep filling in the outline with information from your note cards until you have used up all your cards.

OUTLINE FORM

Thesis statement: _____

_____

_____

Introduction: _____

_____

I. _____

  A. _____

    1. _____

    2. _____

  B. _____

    1. _____

    2. _____

  C. _____

    1. _____

    2. _____

II. _____

  A. _____

    1. _____

    2. _____

B. _____

   1. _____

   2. _____

C. _____

   1. _____

   2. _____

III. _____

  A. _____

   1. _____

   2. _____

  B. _____

   1. _____

   2. _____

  C. _____

   1. _____

   2. _____

Conclusion: _____

_____

CHOOSING A GOOD TITLE

You now have a topic, thesis statement, note cards, and an outline. Your paper is gradually taking shape, so it's time to give it a name. While you might think that a title is one of the last items to work on, many students find that creating a good strong title early helps bring the paper into sharper focus. Creating a title is a short, easy task, and right now, when you are getting ready to plunge into the actual writing of your paper, you need something light and quick to get started.

Since the title page is the first thing your reader will see, a good one should arouse curiosity without being misleading. Think of your title as you would a newspaper or magazine headline. Headlines sell papers. Make sure your title does a good job of selling your research paper even before your reader has a chance to turn the page.

A provocative title does several jobs:

• It indicates the specific subject of the paper.

• It suggests the tone and attitude you have about your paper.

• Above all, it grabs the reader's attention.

There are several types of titles you should consider for your paper. Of course, the kind you choose should suit the purpose of your paper.

1. **Playful titles** give a hint about what your paper is about. They indirectly refer to the topic and arouse the reader's curiosity. To avoid confusion, you can always add an explanatory tag line after the humorous part of the title. Hu-

morous or whimsical titles are often built around a pun or a play on song titles, current sayings, etc. Here are a few examples:

- "Building a Better Mouse" for a paper about how research mice are bred.
- "Going to the Dogs" for a paper on raising pets.
- "Here Comes the Sun" for a paper on solar energy.
- "Rags to Riches" for a paper on the history of blue jeans.
- "Plane Facts" for a paper about the latest in aircraft.

2. **Summary titles** condense the main point of the paper in just a few words. These titles are most like news headlines in that they summarize the facts in a sentence or even less. Here are some examples:

- "Special Effects for Special Movies"
- "Bringing Movies into the Living Room: The Latest in Video Technology"
- "School Vandalism on the Rise"

3. **Preview titles** grab a reader's attention with a question or thought-provoking statement. Examples:

- "Yogurt and Sunflower Seeds Versus the Big Mac: Who's Winning the Food Fight?"
- "The Last Cadillac: Is the Luxury Car Going the Way of the Horse and Buggy?"
- "Who's Minding the Store? Teen Part-Timers Mean Business"

Developing the right title will help you get a slant on the tone of your paper. Spend some time on the wording, considering how the words sound and what they mean.

STEP 7: WRITE THE FIRST DRAFT OF YOUR PAPER

Even experienced writers sometimes get cold feet when it comes to writing down the first sentence. Writer's block shouldn't be a problem for you, however, if you have completed the last six steps in organizing your research paper. When you grouped your note cards and drew up an outline based on your notes, you made important writing decisions about where you were heading with your paper. Since you also have a thesis statement and perhaps a working title, you are already off to a good start.

Your first draft is a question of expanding the basic ideas from your outline, putting them into sentence form, then linking them in an organized way. Think of your first draft as you would a rehearsal for a play or speech. The idea is to run through the basics and work out the fine points later on.

Trying It Out
Goal:
To write a first draft of your research paper

Procedure:
1. Gather your note cards, outline, and a supply of papers and pencils.

2. Look over your thesis statement again. Does it effectively sum up, in a declarative sentence, the main idea of your paper?

3. Check your outline. Is each major topic related to your thesis statement? Does each subtopic support the general topic above it? Are you satisfied that the outline is arranged in logical order? Keep in mind that it's easier to correct problems in your outline now than to rely on making complicated changes in your rough draft later on.

4. Spread out the first group of cards that matches the first heading on your outline. Take the first point from your outline (Roman numeral I) and write a sentence about the main point. Develop that sentence with the information you listed as subtopics in your outline. You can expand these entries by using the details you recorded on the matching note cards for those points. At this stage, don't write down any extensive quotations or passages from the note cards. Either clip the related card to that part of the paper or number-code the card and the section where you plan to add the passage later on.

5. At this point, don't be too concerned about your introduction or conclusion. Many writers work on them after they have developed the body of the paper and have a better idea of what they are introducing or summing up.

6. Leave one or two spaces between each line so that you can add information when you go over your first draft.

7. Write on one side of the page only. This will make it easier for you to flip

through your rough draft when you revise it.

8. As you complete each point in your outline and note cards, check it off to make sure you have included it in your paper.

Progress Check

Fill in the blanks below to see where you are and where you should be heading at this stage. Check with your teacher about problems that crop up.

Where I am so far:
__ have grouped all my note cards by headings that sum up the information on them
__ have made decisions about the sequence in which I plan to use the cards
__ have decided on an organizational pattern or patterns to follow in my paper
__ have written an outline based on the information and organization of my note cards
__ have written a working title for my paper
__ have written the first draft

Problems I'm having:
__ note cards don't seem to tie together
__ can't decide on how to organize cards or outline
__ don't seem to have enough information to support my thesis statement
__ can't get started on my first draft
__ other: _____
_____

Chapter 4

THE BIG FINISH: Revising, Polishing, and Proofreading Your Final Draft

Somewhere in the course of every long writing project comes a moment when the writer is ready to scrap the whole thing. Right about now, you may have the same feeling about your research paper. You've been living with it for several weeks, and it may still seem like a far cry from the neat, polished pages you envisioned when you began the project. At this point, you may even be tempted to simply recopy your rough draft as it stands and hope for the best. Try to resist this urge to wrap up the project quickly. The editing and polishing you do at this point will make the difference between a mediocre paper and a first-rate one.

If you have paced yourself during the last few weeks, you should be able to take a breather from your work schedule for a day or two. You need a cooling-off period so that you can approach your project with a fresh mind when you get to the final stages. The process of revision allows you to stand back from what you've written and evaluate the paper as a whole. To do an effective editing job, you need the perspective that only a break from the work can give you. Even if you only have a couple of days before the final deadline, try to put your paper aside for at least one night so you can get some distance from it.

There are a number of good reasons for devoting as much time to revision as you did to the actual writing of your paper. The first draft established the content and your understanding of the subject. Your later draft or revisions give you a chance to work on the fine points—to fill in any gaps, to provide links between your ideas, and to polish the wording of your language. Moreover, a requirement of most research papers is the acknowledgment of the sources you gathered. This means footnoting quotations, facts, and passages you used in the body of your rough draft, then listing these sources on the bibliography page which you will attach to the end of the paper. Revisions, footnotes, and the bibliography page can be done just before your paper is due.

WRITE THE INTRODUCTION

You may be wondering why this step is slated after the first draft stage. The point of your rough draft was to run through the body of your paper—your main points, supporting ideas, and factual details. As you wrote your first draft, you may have dropped items that were in your original outline and expanded or added others that weren't. Now that all the basic ideas are included in your rough draft, you have a better idea of just exactly what it is that you are introducing.

The introduction is a preview, in condensed form, of everything that follows. It has to do a big job: establish the subject and purpose of the paper, arouse the reader's interest, and make him want to read on. There are a number of ways you can accomplish these goals:

1. **Launch your paper with your thesis statement.** So far, you've been using your thesis statement as the jumping-off point for your research, notes, and outline. Why not start off your paper with it? You may want to reword the statement more provocatively or break it down into several sentences. Since it is the focal point of your paper, your thesis statement is a logical opener. You can then follow it with two or three sentences that describe the aim of your paper.

2. **Begin with a starting fact or statistic from your research.** Your reader will be curious to see how you follow up an intriguing lead.

3. **Borrow an interesting quotation from your notes and use it as an opener.** A well-chosen quotation begins your paper on a note of authority.

4. **Start with an interesting anecdote from your research.** Make your reader interested in following up on the rest of the story.

5. **Raise a question in your introduction.** The right kind of question will encourage your reader to look for the answer in the rest of the paper.

The introduction gives you a chance to point out the value of your research or explain why you have taken a particular position with regard to your topic. Once your introduction has presented your subject in an attention-getting style, it has done its job. So save your supporting statements for the body of your paper.

WRITE THE CONCLUSION

The conclusion recaps your thesis statement and ties up all your major points in a way that leaves your reader feeling satisfied. Keep in mind that it is better to end up with a concise sentence or two than to ramble on for several paragraphs. Think of your conclusion almost as you would a punchline to a joke—if you can't say it quickly and convincingly, you'll lessen the interest you built up earlier.

STEP 8: PROOFREAD AND REVISE YOUR FIRST DRAFT

Look at your rough draft. Perhaps the wording isn't quite what you were reaching for. Maybe the ideas you opened with aren't really as strong as they might be in that spot, while one or two others seem lost where you put them. Or perhaps everything seems in logical order, but somehow your thoughts don't flow quite the way you had hoped. Since the point of your rough draft was to get everything out on paper quickly, you know you'll find spelling and grammatical errors that need correction. With all these possible wrinkles to iron out, how do you go about revising your draft in a systematic way?

First get out your note cards, outline, a note pad, and a red pencil or colored marker for correction. Use these special proofreader's marks to make your job easier:

≡	(capital letter)	These three lines under a letter indicate that the letter should be capitalized.
/	(lower case or split letters or words)	This mark placed through a letter indicates that the letter should be lower case. Placed between two letters it indicates that two words should be formed.
∧	(caret insert)	This mark indicates that a word, phrase, or punctuation mark is being added.
℘	(deletion line)	This mark shows that a word, phrase, or punctuation mark is being taken out.

∽	(letter or word reversal)	This mark shows that two letters or two words should be reversed.
⌣	(connect)	This mark shows that two letters or two words should be joined together.
¶	(paragraph mark)	This mark indicates the need to indent for a new paragraph.
⊙	(period)	This indicates that a period should be added.

As you proofread and revise, you will be reading your paper, preferably aloud, four separate times, so find a quiet place where you can do this in peace.

Checking the Content of Your Paper

During the first reading of your draft, focus on the coverage of your subject by asking yourself these questions:

1. **Is the purpose of your paper clear?** Your teacher will be checking to see how convincing your presentation is. Does your thesis statement come across clearly in the introduction? Is it well-supported with evidence from your research? Does the arrangement of your supporting ideas make your argument come across as effectively as you intended?

2. **Is your paper complete?** You are now an expert on your subject, but your reader probably isn't. Are there any "holes" in the material that

need filling? Any gaps in the amount of information you provide?

3. **Is your information accurate?** If you took careful notes on your cards, this shouldn't be a problem. Just take extra care when you rewrite to make sure you recopy information from your cards word for word.

4. **Is there any irrelevant information?** Don't pad your paper with facts or statements that don't directly tie in with your main purpose. Every piece of information must relate to your thesis statement or you'll lose your reader's attention.

5. **Are your arguments well-supported by facts from your research?** Don't leave your reader hanging; offer factual proof for every generalization or opinion you make.

6. **Is there a focal point to your paper?** Your reader should be able to sum up the point of your paper in a sentence or two if you've gotten across your message effectively.

As you check through the content of your paper, put a number next to each passage in the rough draft that requires a footnote. You will need a footnote for ideas, quotations, and facts that you have borrowed from your research sources. You don't have to include the actual footnote in your rough draft, but later you will coordinate the number you wrote with a corresponding one when you list the actual matching footnote information in your final draft.

Checking the Organization of Your Paper

The organization of your paper is the plan you

had in mind when you grouped your note cards and drew up an outline. In a second reading of your paper, you should be checking to see if your main arguments and ideas flow as smoothly as you thought they would when you developed your outline.

To check on organization, ask yourself these questions and follow the suggested remedies:

1. **Is there a logical beginning, middle, and end to the paper?** If this sequence isn't immediately evident, consider restructuring your material.

2. **Should you change the order of your presentation?** Make sure you state your strongest points early in the paper where they will get the most attention. The most important ideas deserve a proportionate amount of space and the most favorable position in your paper.

3. **Are your ideas arranged and developed in a logical order?** Each paragraph should grow out of the preceding one. Remove any paragraphs or sentences that interrupt the sequence of ideas.

4. **Is the main point of the paper clearly stated in the introduction and summed up in the conclusion?** Reword your opening or ending if they don't do an effective job of presenting or summarizing the aims of your paper.

5. **Does each paragraph develop an idea related to your thesis statement?** Take out any paragraphs that don't directly tie into your main point.

6. **Does each paragraph have a strong topic sentence?** If not, spend time developing sentences that clearly introduce each point you want to make.

7. **Do you provide your reader with connections** to help him shift smoothly from one idea to the next? Transitional words guide the reader from main point to main point. Here is a list of the most widely used connectives:

Connectives Used to Indicate a Time or Spatial Relationship: soon, next, then, later, finally, eventually, first, second, (third, etc.), now, meanwhile, in the meantime, afterward, since, nearby, above, below, beyond, in front (back), to the right (left).

Connectives Used to Indicate a Sequence (to Add Another Thought): and, in addition, also, furthermore, moreover, another, likewise, similarly, next, finally, besides, again, first of all, secondly.

Connectives Used to Indicate Contrast: but, on the other hand, however, rather, nevertheless, otherwise, yet, still, in spite of.

Connectives Used to Indicate Results: therefore, hence, because, thus, consequently, as a result, for, accordingly, so.

Connectives Used to Indicate Examples: for instance, an example of this, for example, take the case of, in other words.

Connectives Used to Indicate Degrees of Certainty: certainly, surely, doubtless, indeed, perhaps, possibly, probably, anyhow, anyway, in all probability, in any case, in all likelihood.

Checking For Style and Tone

Style is the *way* you say something as compared with *what* you say. Your style and tone reveal the attitude you have about your subject. Do you want to be argumentative, persuasive, humorous, or simply informative? You determine the "personality" of your paper when you make certain choices in the wording and structure of the sentences you use. In a research paper, you are speaking from a position of authority about your subject. Therefore the language you use should be somewhat more formal than your tone in an informal essay.

How do you go about developing a definite style for your paper? Here are some questions to ask yourself as you read your draft through a third time:

1. **Is your first paragraph attention-getting?** Try it out on someone else. If it doesn't command interest or arouse curiosity, see if you can change the style and tone of your lead sentences.

2. **Is your vocabulary appropriate to your subject?** If you are writing about the effect of child labor on family life in the early twentieth century, then casual or breezy language would be inappropriate. If the purpose of your paper is to show the changing styles of stand-up comedians in the last ten years, than a looser, more humorous approach is in order.

3. **Do you use strong, active verbs throughout your paper?** The active voice (*e.g.*, "I picked up the phone") gives your writing more strength and energy than the passive voice (*e.g.*, "The phone was picked up").

4. **Do you use specific quotations, examples, and anecdotes to enliven your style?** Back up every general statement you make with specific details. "Ten-year-old children working in garment factories never saw the sun rise or set" is

a stronger, more specific sentence than "Ten-year-old children worked very long hours."

5. **Do you "weave" your quotations smoothly into your own sentences?** Avoid tacking on quotations to your paper; incorporate them into your own style. Here are some tips for doing this:

• Add a quotation to the end of your own sentence. Example: Teenage alcoholics need "a dialogue with their parents."

• Start your own sentence with a phrase from a quotation. Example: ". . . pleased that my son isn't on drugs," one parent preferred to see him drinking a few beers a week instead.

• Use a colon to formally introduce a quotation. Example: Dr. William R. Cunnick, Jr., has said: "Many parents feel pleased that their kids are not on angel dust or heroin and 'only using' alcohol."

Short quotations (four or five lines) are worked into your paper with quotations marks and are followed by a footnote number at the end of the quotation. Quotations that are longer than five lines are set apart in a separate paragraph, ending with a footnote number.

6. **Do you vary your choice of words and phrases?** Use your dictionary and thesaurus to locate variations of similar terms and expressions.

7. **Do you vary your sentence structure and paragraph openings?** Unless you do, your paper will have a sing-song quality that will bore your reader.

8. **Is your style compact and concise?** Choose the simple word and phrase rather than the most complicated, the most economical way of saying

something rather than the most drawn-out.

Proofread for Grammar and Mechanics

You have now read over your rough draft for content, organization, and style. Use your last reading to check grammar, spelling, punctuation, and capitalization. As you read aloud this last time, make sure there are no missing or extra words. Keep your dictionary handy to check on any spelling you aren't sure about. Use your grammar book or a style sheet from English class to look up any grammatical questions you have.

Here is what you should be looking for as you read your draft at this stage:

1. All paragraphs are indented.

2. All sentences begin with a capital letter.

3. All sentences are correctly punctuated.

4. All quotations are noted with quotation marks.

5. All spelling is correct.

6. All verbs agree with the subject in tense and number.

7. Verb tenses and pronoun agreement are consistent.

Writing Footnotes

You know those tiny lines of type you never read at the bottom of textbook pages or nonfiction books? Those are footnotes. They tell you the source of any quoted or excerpted information.

To avoid plagiarism—that is, the theft of another writer's ideas—authors who use facts, opinions, and statements from outside sources acknowledge them by placing a raised number next to the borrowed material and a corresponding number at the foot of the page. Next to the bottom number, they write down the author's name, the title, and the page of the borrowed material.

There are a few simple rules to keep in mind when you do your own footnotes:

• Number footnotes consecutively for the whole paper.

• Place the footnote just above the end of the cited statement. (See sample research paper in the last chapter for examples of how to do this.)

• Write your footnote information below a two-inch line that separates the body of your paper from your footnote list.

• If the author is not known, write the title of the work first.

• If you repeat a source used earlier, just list the last name of the author followed by the Latin words, *Op. Cit.* ("already mentioned") and the new page number. Use the Latin phrase *Ibid.* ("in the same place") if the source is immediately above it and the page number is the same as in the previous footnote.

Here is a sampling of footnotes shown in the research paper included in the last chapter of this book:

1. Leo B. Kneer, *Science Fact/Fiction*, p. 75.
2. Douglas Colligan, "Robots: Mechanized Slaves Come of Age," *Science Digest*, p. 35.
3. Goran Lundstrom, *Industrial Robots*, p. 92.
4. *Op. Cit.*, p. 95.
5. Fred Reed, "The Robots Are Coming, the Robots Are Coming," *Next*, p. 32.
6. Colligan, "Robots: Mechanized Slaves Come of Age," p. 37

Trying It Out

Goal:

To acknowledge, in footnotes, all the sources you used in your research paper.

Procedure:

1. Have your bibliography and note cards on hand. Then read your rough draft. When you come across a borrowed fact, quotation, idea, or other piece of information from your research, put a small number at the end of the sentence in which the information appears.

2. Write a corresponding number at the bottom of the page.

3. When you write your final draft, fill in the footnote information next to each number at the bottom of the page. Follow the footnote rules mentioned in this chapter. You will get all your footnote information from your bibliography and note cards.

Preparing the Bibliography Page

The bibliography is a list of all the books and materials you used to prepare your paper. You attach it at the end of your final draft. All the information for the bibliography comes from the bibliography cards you prepared. Here is how a typical bibliography page for a research paper is arranged:

BIBLIOGRAPHY

Asimov, Isaac, *Caves of Steel*, New York, Doubleday, 1970.

Browning, Iban, and Robert Winkless, *Robots on Your Doorstep*, New York, Robotics Press, 1978.

Colligan, Douglas, "The Robots Are Coming," *New York Magazine*, 12:30 (July 30, 1979), 40-44.

———, "Robots: Mechanized Slaves Come of Age," *Science Digest*, 75 (June, 1974), 34-39.

Freeman, Michael, and Gary Mulkowsky, "Robots in the Home and Classroom," *The Futurist*, XII:6 (December, 1978), 358-361.

Kneer, Leo B., *Science Fact/Fiction*, New York, Scott, Foresman and Co., 1974.

Lundstrom, Goran, *Industrial Robots*, New York, Scholim International, 1972.

Malone, Robert, *The Robot Book*, New York, Harcourt, Brace Jovanovich, 1978.

Post, Jonathan V., "Cybernetic War," *Omni*, I:8 (May, 1979), 45-52.

Reed, Fred, "The Robots Are Coming, the Robots Are Coming," *Next*, 1:2 (May/June, 1980), 30-38.

Trying It Out

Goal:

To prepare the bibliography page for the final draft of your own research paper.

Procedure:

1. Arrange your bibliography cards alphabetically by the last name of the author who wrote each book or article you used in researching your paper. (If you don't have the name of an author, alphabetize

by the first main word of a magazine article or book title.)

2. Use a reverse-indentation form where the author's name is flush with the left-hand margin and the information below the name is indented five spaces or so.

3. Copy down the information from your bibliography cards on a sheet of paper in the alphabetized order in which you arranged the cards.

4. If you used two works by the same author, simply put a line where the author's name would be, followed by the title and publication information of the source.

STEP 9: WRITE THE FINAL DRAFT

At this point you have edited and marked your rough draft for content, organization, style, and mechanics. You have footnoted borrowed material and prepared a bibliography sheet. The final assembly of your paper is simply a matter of neatly recopying or typing the corrected draft. You must also add a title page and page numbers, and attach your bibliography sheet.

STEP 10: ASSEMBLE AND PROOFREAD THE FINAL DRAFT

Trying It Out

Goal:

To assemble your final paper.

Procedure:

1. Recopy your corrected draft neatly, incorporating all the changes you made when you edited and proofread it. By all means, type your paper if you are a good typist. It will make a favorable impression on your teacher who will be reading through dozens of research papers.

2. Prepare a title page that includes this information:

TITLE

(in all caps if typed)

by

Your Name

Course

Teacher

Date

3. Write in all the footnote information where you indicated footnote numbers in your rough draft.

4. Number your paper consecutively from the first page (not including the title page) right through to the bibliography page.

5. Proofread your paper carefully one last time.

6. Staple or clip the paper together and submit it on or before the due date.

Congratulations! You're finished. Sit back and relax. It's your teacher's turn to do the hard work now. If you followed the recommended steps in this book, the job of correcting your paper will be an easy one.

When you get back your paper, look over the teacher's corrections and comments carefully. Save your research paper to use as a model for the many term papers you will be writing in the upper grades or later on in college.

Chapter 5

RESEARCH PAPER SURVIVAL KIT

ANOTHER KIND OF TERM PAPER

You have learned how to produce a long-term, formal research paper based on library sources. From time to time, however, it's also fun to work on assignments that involve other kinds of research — interviews, surveys, comparison tests, or simple fact-checking. Below are a number of topics you can develop without necessarily going to the library. Depending on the topic, your research may involve designing questionnaire forms, conducting taped interviews, going through old newspapers or microfilm, visiting government archives, historical societies, and local cemeteries, or writing away to geneological services. Why not try you hand at one of these unusual term projects for your next big writing assignment?

1. Research and write your family history.

2. Draw a family tree.

3. Write a report on the current events of the day and week in which you were born.

4. Make up a time line on a subject that interests you.

5. Survey classmates, friends, neighbors, or family members about topics and trends that interest you (allowances, buying habits, curfews, entertainment preferences, team favorites, tastes in food or clothes, pet peeves, etc.). Write a report based on your findings.

6. Research and write a report on the meaning and origins of the first names of everyone in your class.

7. Test and compare two or three brands of a common product.

8. Make up a "Top 10" list for popular current records, television shows, movies, foods, etc. based on surveys of friends, classmates, and family members.

9. Create a personalized calendar, diary, or date book on a subject that interests you (astrology signs, celebrity birthdays, famous dates in music, films, literature, etc.).

10. Interview older family members of various ages to compare aspects of teenage life then and now. Write up a comparison of contemporary and past teen customs.

11. Survey friends about what a Utopian teen town would be like and write a report based on your findings.

12. Interview family members about courtship customs going back several decades.

13. Survey classmates to find out what they would do if they won $100,000, and write a report on the results.

14. Make up a map plotting the journeys of grandparents, aunts, uncles, and cousins.

15. If you are interested in photography, gather as many old family pictures as you can from relatives near and far. Duplicate the pictures and make up a visual family history based on the pictures.

16. Interview older family members and neighbors, then, in a report, reconstruct their impressions of what your hometown was like a long time ago.

17. Visit a local cemetery and reconstruct the lives of people buried there based on engravings on the gravestones.

18. Interview family members or several classmates about an important event in their lives, then put together a "newspaper" complete with headlines about each of those events.

19. Contact people working in professions that interest you and see if you can arrange to interview some of them. Then write a report describing what you learned about their work and how you can prepare for that profession.

20. Browse through an encyclopedia chapter and some travel books describing a country that appeals to you. Then write up an itinerary for a one-month trip to that country, imagining that you had ample funds to finance such a journey.

150 RESEARCH PAPER TOPICS

Your best bet in selecting an interesting research paper subject is to explore your own interests. At the same time, you may find it helpful to read through a listing of general subject areas to get started.

Listed on the following pages are 150 general topics. Your final selection, of course, will be affected by the availability of adequate research sources in your library, your ability to narrow down one of these general subjects to a size suitable for a junior high or high school research paper, and your teacher's approval. With these considerations in mind, look over this listing and see if there's any area you would like to investigate for your research paper.

Architecture — Engineering
1. the world's longest bridges
2. the world's tallest buildings
3. Egypt's pyramids
4. Frank Lloyd Wright's private houses
5. crazy inventions
6. the building of the first railroads through the American West
7. underground houses
8. cars that never hit the road
9. flying machines that never got off the ground
10. cities in space

Art
11. prehistoric cave art
12. art of the American Indians
13. career of a famous artist

14. American folk art in furniture and decoration
15. careers in graphic and commercial art
16. the childhoods of famous artists
17. photography as an artform
18. medieval stained-glass windows
19. decorative arts (pottery, jewelry, fabric, glass, etc.)
20. Egyptian art

Animals
21. most poisonous animals
22. animal language
23. exotic pets
24. pet food industry
25. famous movie animals
26. eating habits of domestic pets
27. rare animals
28. endangered animals making a comeback
29. laws governing endangered animals
30. children raised by animals

Aviation
31. Charles Lindbergh's transatlantic flight
32. famous airplane disasters
33. balloon flights
34. World War II aviators and their planes
35. planes that never got off the ground

Believe It or Not
36. famous haunted houses
37. famous ghosts
38. real-life coincidences
39. great survival stories
40. dangerous occupations

41. bizarre natural disasters
42. famous disappearances
43. UFOs
44. Loch Ness, Bigfoot, and all those other animals
45. origins of common superstitions

Education
46. unusual schools
47. dress codes and other school rules around the country
48. education then and now (compare what school was like for students your age in another time)
49. the first public schools
50. successful people who never graduated from high school

Entertainment
51. early days of television
52. quiz show scandals in the 1950s
53. new television technology
54. writers who became comedians
55. famous movie monsters
56. the Academy Awards
57. the arrival of the talkies
58. the history of the famous movie studios
59. the development of movie special effects
60. child stars of the '40s and '50s

Government and the Law
61. famous political scandals
62. crazy laws
63. the rights of students and minors
64. landmark cases in education

65. famous trials in history
66. first women politicians
67. voter polls
68. the selling of a politician in the media
69. great political debates
70. U.S. immigration policies during various periods

Labor
71. careers to explore or avoid in the next ten years
72. child-labor laws in the early twentieth century
73. teenage entrepreneurs
74. the first U.S. labor strikes
75. who picks the nation's fruit and vegetables

Mystery and Crime
76. famous unsolved murders
77. famous heists
78. notorious outlaws of the '20s and '30s
79. famous spies
80. great escapes
81. famous forgers, frauds, and phonies
82. notorious gangs and outlaws in the Old West
83. unsolved kidnappings
84. famous fictional detectives and their techniques
85. life of a famous mystery writer

Popular Culture
86. the history of blue jeans
87. fads that came and went
88. dance styles of the last thirty years

89. famous comic-book heroes
90. the growth of fast food
91. media trivia
92. the history of the chocolate bar
93. the social life of teenagers then and now
94. the fabulous (or not-so-fabulous) '50s or '60s
95. whatever happened to the 1970s
96. history of famous products
97. rites of passage for teenagers in different cultures
98. history of our funeral, wedding, or birth customs
99. social etiquette then and now
100. how the nation vacations

Literature and Language
101. changing forms of slang
102. name origins
103. great romances in literature
104. Nobel- and Pulitzer-prizewinners — what they had in common
105. habits of famous writers — how they work
106. teenage lives of famous writers
107. people whose names became everyday words
108. famous quotations and the stories behind them
109. the most popular children's books
110. what's happening to people's reading habits

Music
111. composers and musicians who died young
112. history of rock-and-roll

113. history of soul music
114. gospel music and rhythm-and-blues
115. the effect of rock-and-roll on politics, styles, and other kinds of music

Science and Technology
116. weather predictions
117. research in psychic phenomena
118. lost cities and civilizations
119. spy and killer satellites
120. active volcanoes
121. disastrous oil spills
122. how certain everyday objects work
123. the growth of computers in everyday life
124. future foods
125. cities of the future
126. firefighting techniques
127. microsurgery
128. use of lasers in medicine
129. robots — their history and future
130. black holes

Sports
131. the Olympic games
132. great moments in sports
133. sports oddities
134. great automobile races
135. the physical fitness craze
136. invention of a particular sport or game
137. baseball then and now
138. television and sports
139. broken records — how records were broken in a particular sport
140. sports scandals

Grab Bag

141. left-handers
142. changing life expectancies in the last century
143. how the nation spends its free time
144. whatever happened to . . . (celebrities of yesteryear)
145. myths and facts about the Old West
146. turning points in men's and women's fashions
147. where did the dinosaurs go
148. how to become an astronaut
149. whatever happened to the famous hippies
150. child prodigies in science, music, or sports

SAMPLE RESEARCH PAPER

ROBOTS IN
FACT AND FICTION

by

John A. Halvorsen

English 4
Third Period
Mr. John Murphy
March 1, 1981

Few machines get as much attention in fiction, both on the movie screen and between the covers of a novel, as does the robot. The role it plays is usually one of three kinds: a villain, an ultra-intelligent hero, a sidekick to the hero. Now that science and technology have advanced to the point where they are populating the world with genuine robots, it appears that robots are destined to be neither mechanical villains nor heroes. From all the evidence now in, it looks as though the twentieth-century robot, the robot of fact, is only a dimly intelligent mechanical slave. What effect this dumb machine will have on our future is debatable, with no agreement among the experts.

Since the robot first appeared as a creature of fiction, it is a good idea to start with the kinds of preconceptions the make-believe robots created. The modern history of the fictional robot began with a play, called *R.U.R.*, written in 1921 by the Czechoslovakian playwright, Karel Capek. The play was a kind of science-fiction allegory in which Capek introduced the word "robot." Taken from a Slavic word meaning "work," robot was Capek's name for lifelike mechanical men manufactured by a company called Rossum's Universal Robots which, in abbreviated form, is the play's title.

In the play, the more intelligent robots organized a revolt, rose up against the humans who made them, and in the end killed all but one. The character who was allowed to survive (because, like the robots, he worked with his hands) muttered over and over the line which summed up the spirit of the play: "It was a crime to make robots."[1]

That is one typical theme of robot fiction —
the machine that turns on its maker. The other,
more optimistic one, appears in several of Isaac
Asimov's books. In them, he portrays androids,
uncannily built robots so lifelike they look human to the untrained eye. Asimov's robots are
loyal, intelligent, and totally selfless. (A typical
plot unfolds in *The Caves of Steel*. A police officer/
robot named R. Daneel Olivaw helps his human
police partner, Lije Baley, solve a homicide ap-
parently committed by a robot.)

In Asimov's science-fiction world, robots are
incapable of any harm to humans because of
their robot conscience, based on Asimov's Three
Laws of Robotics:

1. A robot may not injure a human
   being, or through inaction allow a human being to come to harm.
2. A robot must obey the orders given
   it by human beings, except where such
   orders would conflict with the First Law.
3. A robot must protect its own exis-
   tence, except where such protection
   would conflict with the First or Second
   Law.[2]

These, in brief, are samples of two standard
fictional treatments of the robot in modern life.
Since science fact has now caught up to fiction
a little, there is evidence that the real life of the
modern robot follows a third, less obvious plot
line: the robot as the dimwitted but efficient
worker-drone.

---

1. Leo B. Kneer, *Science Fact/Fiction*, p. 75.
2. Isaac Asimov, *Caves of Steel*, p. 35

Right now there are robots at work all over the United States and even all over the solar system. Car manufacturers such as General Motors have been using robots for years to do the routine assembly line work of welding and spray-painting cars.[3] The U.S. military has been using robots to do dangerous or sometimes humanly impossible work. At one arms depot in Utah, for example, a robot handles the ticklish job of disarming complex bombs.[4] The military makes heavy use of robot spy-in-the-sky satellites, such as the notorious "Big Bird" satellite with its incredibly sharp camera lens used to photograph Soviet military bases from space.[5]

Robots have been frequently used in space missions. The Soviet Union has landed several Lunokhods, wheeled robots, on the surface of the moon, and the United States put a very sophisticated robot, the Viking Lander, on the surface of Mars.[6]

Here on earth there are office buildings where the mail is delivered several times each day by robot delivery carts, and one man even built a robot to help his wife teach her third-grade class.[7] The robot would go over lesson drills with some students in the back of the class while the human teacher would instruct the rest of the class in the front. As clever and sophisticated

3. Goran Lundstrom, *Industrial Robots*, p. 92.

4. *Op. Cit.*, p. 95.

5. Fred Reed, "The Robots Are Coming, the Robots Are Coming," *Next*, (May/June, 1980), p. 32

6. Colligan, "Robots: Mechanized Slaves Come of Age," *Science Digest*, (June, 1974), p. 37

7. Michael Freeman and Gary Mulkowsky, "Robots in the Home and Classroom," *The Futurist*, (December, 1978), p. 359

as some of these machines are, none of them even remotely resembles the kinds of robots that surface in fiction.

To begin with, none has that most dangerous of fictional robot abilities: a mind of its own. The less "intelligent" robots are constantly guided via remote control by humans who think through their every move for them. The more elaborate models have a small memory system which trains them to do very simple jobs unattended. The problem is they will do the same thing over and over mindlessly until they are turned off or simply wear out. Even what has been called the "most complex robot ever constructed," the Viking Lander that went to Mars, needed no laws of robotics to keep it in line.[8]

The Viking Lander was an ingenious creation of scientists who wanted to get first-hand information about the surface of Mars without risking the life of an astronaut. The Lander was a self-contained laboratory and communications center. It had a telescopic arm which was used to reach out and scoop up a sample of Martian dirt. The soil would be dropped inside the robot, which would run it through a battery of tests, then radio the results back to Earth. "As incredibly versatile as it is, it does not begin to approach the complexity of a human being — it is just not in the same league," notes robot expert Robert Malone.[9] Unlike its fictional counterparts, the Viking had no robot mind of its own. When it had done its job, it just clicked off and was left stranded on Mars.

---

8. Robert Malone, *The Robot Book*, p. 96.
9. *Op. Cit.*, p. 84.

Today's robots not only don't have much of human intellect, they don't even have very human shapes. What they do determines how they look. The Viking Lander, for example, looked like a squat, three-legged insect. It was made low and compact to fit inside the rocket that carried it to Mars. According to one writer, industrial robots are "just arms mounted on boxes."[10] The robot that acts as a mail deliverer is an ordinary-looking cart that can do extraordinary things. It can call its own elevators and follow an invisible chemical track on a carpeted floor using a special ultraviolet sensor built into its belly. But no one looking at it would guess it was a robot.

Besides lacking a human mind and body, the robots which now exist also lack two basic skills humans take for granted. A three-year-old child can reach into a basket and pick out his or her favorite toy. The sleek, sophisticated twentieth-century robot, with its miniaturized circuitry and computerized guidance, cannot. Modern robots are blind and have no sense of touch. For example, if no cars were coming down the production line and the industrial robots were left running, they would continue to weld and spray-paint empty air.

The robot cannot see what is out of place, nor can it pull something into proper position, so, if things aren't where they should be, the machine becomes totally confused. Robot builders have made sight and touch the big goals of robot research but, as they are finding out, teaching a machine to recognize an object the way hu-

10. Reed, p. 32.

mans do is not easy. One robot expert says that they have to distill a picture into information points that could make sense to a machine. This is a complex job. Even a fuzzy television picture can have as many as 275,000 information points which the robot has to process in a matter of seconds.[11] And as for the hand, one experienced builder of industrial robots says giving a machine something with the versatility of the human hand is an equally difficult engineering challenge.[12]

Although the robots of fact neither think like humans nor look like humans, nor even have some of the most basic human skills, there are signs that the humanization of the machine is slowly happening. At one bank where the robot cart is used, the machine has been given a whole list of nicknames by its human co-workers: Jo Jo, the Monster, and Tinkerbell, to name three.[13]

Of a little more significance is what happened to the robot one man built to help teach a grammar-school class. His classroom model was, in fact, a talking computer, but was purposely shaped like the standard science-fiction robot to draw the children to it. More important, the robot had a "personality," actually just a prerecorded group of responses — jokes, comments, questions — that a very patient teacher with a good sense of humor might use. That single talking robot became so popular, a toy company adapted the design for a small, plastic teaching

11. Colligan, "Robots: Mechanized Slaves Come of Age," p. 39.

12. Reed, p. 34.

13. Colligan, "The Robots Are Coming," *New York Magazine,* (July 30, 1979), p. 44.

robot it sold in toy stores all over the country.

Like the original, the toy, called 2-XL, has a "personality," which, in the best science-fiction tradition, was designed for it by a panel of psychologists and other behavioral scientists. To keep a child interested in a subject, the robot teaches from a prerecorded eight-track tape. The little machine tells jokes, laughs, compliments a learner when he's right, and sounds disappointed when the child is wrong.[14]

Inventions like this are nudging the dumb, patient robot of today in the general direction of the fictional robot. It is conceivable that the robots people once only made up stories about could appear soon enough.

Robot watchers today are not worried about the threat from the sophisticated robot the way it is usually portrayed: the creature turning on its creator. They are worried about a more subtle danger: what the robot slave of the future could do to the mind and spirit of people in the years to come. As one expert warns: "The speed with which we can expect the widespread introduction of the robot to proceed will be the real problem. Human beings will have little time to adapt slowly to the robotic revolution."[15] Adding to this, another writer says: "These robots will be doing more and more things that humans now do. We may begin to feel that they are intruding in almost every aspect of our lives."[16]

This is probably the most critical difference between the robots of fiction and those of fact.

14. Freeman and Mulkowsky, p. 357.

15. Iban Browning and Robert Winkless, *Robots on Your Doorstep*, p. 291.

16. Malone, p. 9.

It is a more insidious threat than something like an android revolution and has some of the elements of the happy-ending version of the robot as friend, not enemy. The question it raises is: What will happen to a society where machines do more and more and humans do less and less? Will people become more creative or just lazier? These questions cannot be answered yet, but one that can is what will happen to jobs. Men and machines could be competing for the same work and, in some instances, the human could lose out.

Unions agree that robots have, in all likelihood, permanently replaced humans on some assembly line jobs, but few people are complaining since they are not prestigious positions.[17] Similarly, the bank in New York City which began using robots instead of humans cut down on the number of people it uses for those jobs, just one more instance where, this time in a white-collar setting, another machine became one of the workers.[18]

Futuristic thinkers say life could get even more complex in the future. One engineer with the National Bureau of Standards believes it would be conceivable to build a factory entirely run by robots. They would not only manufacture products, they would also be able to rebuild and replace other robot workers that wore out — all within the confines of the factory. It could be the start of a whole robot-worker economy.

Whether this will actually happen is debatable. Some robot experts point out that robots are

17. Reed, p. 36.
18. Colligan, "The Robots Are Coming," p. 44.

not always the best workers for a job, either because they are too expensive for the job or cannot be trained to do certain jobs that require fine coordination — watch repair or surgery, for example.

For the time being, however, it does not appear that we humans will be faced with the science-fiction idea of the robot as friend or robot as enemy but, if current trends continue, the robot as obedient, tireless slave. This third situation is more interesting and more volatile because, depending on how humans react to them, the robots have the potential of turning into either the monsters or the helpers science fiction has been warning us about for years.

BIBLIOGRAPHY

Asimov, Isaac, *Caves of Steel*, New York, Doubleday, 1970.

Browning, Iban, and Robert Winkless, *Robots on Your Doorstep*, New York, Robotics Press, 1978.

Colligan, Douglas, "The Robots Are Coming," *New York Magazine*, 12:30 (July 30, 1979), 40-44.

————, "Robots: Mechanized Slaves Come of Age," *Science Digest*, 75 (June, 1974), 34-39.

Freeman, Michael, and Gary Mulkowsky, "Robots in the Home and Classroom," *The Futurist*, XII:6 (December, 1978), 358-361.

Kneer, Leo B., *Science Fact/Fiction*, New York, Scott, Foresman and Co., 1974.

Lundstrom, Goran, *Industrial Robots*, New York, Scholim International, 1972.

Malone, Robert, *The Robot Book*, New York, Harcourt, Brace Jovanovich, 1978.

Post, Jonathan V., "Cybernetic War," *Omni*, I:8 (May, 1979), 45-52.

Reed, Fred, "The Robots Are Coming, the Robots Are Coming," *Next*, 1:2 (May/June, 1980), 30-38.

RESEARCH PAPER SCHEDULE

Research

Jobs to be done:	Due Dates:	Check-off:
1. Think of a general subject that interests you.	___	___
2. Narrow your general subject down to a specific subtopic.	___	___
3. Go to the library and see what information is available on your topic. Make a list of all usable research sources on bibliography cards.	___	___
4. Take notes on the materials you listed. Record your research on note cards.	___	___
5. Write a thesis statement that sums up the main point of your paper and the research you have uncovered so far.	___	___

Organizing Your Paper

6. Read over your note cards and decide which information you would like to include or omit. _____ _____

7. Arrange your note cards in logical order. _____ _____

8. Write an outline based on the arrangement of your note cards. _____ _____

Writing Your Paper

9. Write a rough draft of your paper, main point by main point, from your outline and note cards. Support each main idea with facts, examples, and subtopics from your note cards. _____ _____

10. Work on the introduction and conclusion of your paper. _____ _____

11. Go over your rough draft to see if all your ideas relate to one another and to your thesis statement. Check that you've

supported all your main ideas with researched facts and examples. Polish the style of your rough draft. _____ _____

12. Rewrite your rough draft into a final copy. Document facts, quotations, and passages with footnotes. Write up a bibliography sheet from your bibliography cards. _____ _____

13. Proofread your final draft for mechanics and neatness. _____ _____

14. Submit your paper on the due date. _____ _____

OUTLINE FORM

Thesis statement: _____

_____

_____

Introduction: _____

_____

I. _____

   A. _____

      1. _____

      2. _____

   B. _____

      1. _____

      2. _____

   C. _____

      1. _____

      2. _____

II. _____

   A. _____

      1. _____

      2. _____

   B. _____

      1. _____

      2. _____

   C. _____

      1. _____

      2. _____

III. _____

  A. _____

    1. _____

    2. _____

  B. _____

    1. _____

    2. _____

  C. _____

    1. _____

    2. _____

Conclusion: _____
_____

A RESEARCH PAPER CHECKLIST

Organization:

☐ There is a logical beginning, middle, and end to my paper.

☐ The main point of my paper is clearly stated in the introduction and summed up in the conclusion.

☐ Each paragraph develops an idea related to my main topic.

☐ Each paragraph has a strong topic sentence.

☐ All opinions are supported with facts and examples.

Grammar:

☐ I have indented all paragraphs.

☐ I have used capital letters to begin all sentences.

☐ I have correctly punctuated all sentences.

☐ I have used only complete sentences.

☐ I have checked the spelling.

☐ I have checked that all verbs agree with the subject.

☐ I have kept verb tenses consistent.

Mechanics:

☐ I have included a cover for the research paper that lists the title, my name, the date, and my class.

☐ I have left margins on all sides of each sheet of paper for teacher corrections.

☐ I have numbered each page of my research paper.

☐ I have included a bibliography of my research sources at the end of the paper.

☐ I have written as clearly and neatly as possible.

INDEX